My workbook

Presented to: ______________________________

Address: ______________________________

____

Birthdate: ______________________________

Spiritual
Birthdate: ______________________________

Please use this wisely, it is meant to be a source of great wealth in every area of your life. You may pick this up years after you have started recording info into it, and it will bring you back. This tool is precious and timeless. It may be the legacy that you pass on to the future generations of your family. Please store in a safe place and remember to use it as a diary of your growth. We know that after following the techniques you will be amazed everyday with your relationship with our Father, God.

This timeless gift is from those who love you!

____

____

____

An Instrument for God's Purpose

By David J. DesBois

We are all works in progress, in the process of being tuned and played in the great commission. The hardest part is to just let go and fall into our Lord's arms. The hope is that our consciousness of our Father grows through His word. His love envelopes us and gives strength through every moment.

www.facebook.com/pages/Let-Your-Light-Shine

livinglovinglordsheart blogspot.com

Published by Net2church Global Ministries

www.Net2Church.org

david.j.desbois@gmail.com

ISBN 978-1-105-55637-1

First Printing

Published by Net2church Global Ministries

www.Net2Church.org

Printed in the United States of America

By www.LULU.com

Appreciations

Thank you to all that helped make this workbook what it is and the blessing it will be.

First is my wife Linda. Her support and faith in me has given me the strength to overcome many obstacles. She opened my heart.

My niece Lori Deaton took an idea and turned it into a work of art which is the cover.

Special thanks to all the pastors, writers and friends that reviewed the rough draft. Their insights brought clarity and simplicity to this work.

David and Rhonda Thayer gave hospitality and love. They opened their home to me, did tremendous editing work, and supported me when I needed it the most.

Also Devin Thayer and his computer work that helped organize the material and his computer which I used to write.

Thanks and praise to God for He gets all the glory. We are nothing without Him.

CONTENT

INTRODUCTION

Who are we as children of God, (the God of the universe)? What is our Father like? How should we walk and talk knowing the power that is inside of us? Jesus is our Lord, brother, and example. Do we resemble Him in our daily walk? At what stage are we in our maturity, meaning our likeness to God? What or how do we take action to mature? Do we keep track of our work and growth? What are the meanings of words and their power in our lives?

This short workbook is a tool to be used to help answer the above questions. Growth is a process, either conscious or unconscious, towards the many levels of maturity. Faith or unbelief grows in direct relation to our decisions and actions. The Word says that we are to hunger and thirst after righteousness. This book is based on 27 years of a personal search, along with wisdom and techniques from fellow Christians' preaching, teaching and books planted in my heart. We are in the end times and do not have time to fumble around blindly to maturity. As believers, we are called to listen to our teacher (The Holy Spirit), obey our Father (God), and fall in love with our Lord and Savior (Jesus).

Whether you buy this book or not, I pray that your eyes of understanding will be enlightened to who you are. Also the promises you have as a child of God, excite you to thankfulness and praise. That the joy and peace which surpasses understanding spring up in your heart. Also that you taste the excitement and thrill of helping God bring someone into His Kingdom, permitting God to use you as An Instrument for God's Purpose.

DEDICATION

I heard a story many years ago, which I just now remembered, today 2/11 at 7:30 pm. "All heaven stood quiet and still. Then you could hear the angels say "she is coming, she is coming, she is coming". Who could this woman be which caused all heaven to stand still? We just saw pastors meet Jesus with their 100's and 1,000's of followers and families. Also Evangelist, Prophets and Teachers with 1,000's and 10,000's of thousands of souls won into the kingdom. As I pondered this thought, there I saw her. She was a petite, white haired woman walking slowly but extremely deliberately and powerfully. Behind her were 100,000's of thousands of people following. There were pastors by the dozens, missionaries, evangelist, prophets and many, many, saints with the same glow she emanated. Who was this woman and what had she done? I asked some angels present. Oh, they said, she released us on many powerful assignments and held back the forces of evil as we accomplished our missions. She is a fervent, steadfast and committed intercessory prayer. She worked hand in hand with Jesus while He is seated at the right hand of God.

This story explains those to whom I would like to dedicate this book. For all the prayer intercessors, especially my spiritual mother Beverly Long, my brother and fellow intercessor partner Scott Manseau, my former pastor Kerry Twing who has gone to be with the Lord. Also my grandmother Mary DesBois who, I know, was praying for me as I grew physically and spiritually.

PRELUDE

Many of us, who are Christians and have been for years, took years to mature to where we are. We are still children in relation to God, and Jesus is our big brother. Many are striving, but still have not reached the fullness of maturity. God states in His word "there is sin that so easily entangles us... He also says "...to put it aside." These could be physical bad habits, un-forgiveness, laziness, apathy, lack of faith, or any human weakness. God will reveal to the individual where and what they may be as they continue in the process to be closer to Him. Some have matured to a point and are walking closer with God and His purpose on this Earth. If you ask them or watch their walk, they would humbly say or reveal that their process continues. {As I was thinking about this thought I walked out on my deck and four Canadian geese flew by. Three were flying in perfect alignment and one was coming up behind. Revelation came at that moment. The Father, Son, and Holy Spirit are in perfect alignment and flying effortlessly. The one coming up behind is us working to join them.} What amazed me was the perfect timing of the event. I was out on the deck at the precise time that the four geese flew by. God is Amazing!

For new Christians, you are babies, this is a fact, so do not be offended. We love you more than you know right now. You need to feed on the pure milk of the Word. This book is an energized formula, which will catapult you to a quicker enlightenment and revelation of God and your relation to Him! You will need to find a fellowship to attend. A good indication that a church has God and the Holy Spirit in it is not the music but rather the love the brothers have one to another. Also is the entire Bible preached and taught as the word of God? Jesus, is he lifted up as the son of God? Then find a mature Christian that is willing to mentor you. (Yes, as a more mature Christian, you should be willing to take a youngster under your wings and be that helper.) I stress, do not hesitate to ask a mature brother or sister in the Lord to help you grow in the Word. This book is only a supplement.

This book, inspired by God, is jumper cables or a vitamin for those of us who have been Christians for years. Many times we get so active in church or good works that we walk right past the most important part of being a Christian. Our first love, the relationship, intimate relationship with God, which He so desires. In the book of Revelation the churches are reprimanded for leaving their first love 'Jesus'. We go to church, get preached to, great scriptures and messages, but walk away somewhat empty. The spiritual food is good and our spirit does get fed, but something is missing. How can I receive a deeper more conscious relationship with God? What is missing? I have been going to church and Bible studies over and over again; still I am not walking in the maturity and fullness of Jesus Christ. Jesus stated to his followers, “the works that I have done, you will do and even greater works.” Using that as the gauge, are we there yet? Honestly, we would all have to say, **no**. Is that a realistic goal? Yes. Because Jesus said it, it is the truth.

THE RIGHT GUITAR

The first step in tuning up a guitar is to make sure you are the right guitar. Are you a son or daughter of the God of the universe? The God of Abraham, the God that delivered the Israelites out of Egypt, Creator of Heaven and Earth, and the Father of Jesus Christ of Nazareth, the Lamb of God, (our Redeemer). Are you positively absolutely sure deep down in your heart that you are a child of God? That is in your inner man, which may be compared to knowing how to ride a bike, tie your shoes or even walk. You know how to do these things without even thinking about them. This is the kind of knowing that I am talking about. If you do, you may skip the next chapter and proceed with the process of tuning your guitar. If not I would like to share with you some good news. This will transform your life from walking in the darkness to total transparency of light of understanding.

The God that created all things, you included, loves you very much. His will is that you have fellowship with him on a personal basis as he did with Adam and Eve. God walked and talked with Adam in the Garden but there was a great division and death entered the world; (Genesis 2 & 3). God made a way to reunite His creation, you, with himself through His son Jesus. You will find this in the Bible in John 3:16 and Romans 10: 9, 10. You may get a Bible and read them for yourself. We will be referring to the Bible (Basic Instructions before Leaving Earth) many times in this book. At this time I would like you to take this opportunity to introduce you to the greatest friend you will ever have. As you say these words, if you will believe them with your heart, you will be born again.

Jesus, come into my life, forgive me
of all my sins. I ask you to cleanse
my heart and make me a new person
in you right now. I believe that you
are the Son of God and that you died
on the cross for me. Jesus, I want to
thank you for loving me enough to die

for me. I accept all that your shed
blood bought for me on the cross and
I receive you as my Savor and Lord.
In your name I pray. Amen

After praying this prayer and believing in your heart, congratulations! You are born again, a new creature in Christ and as 2 Corinthians 5:17 says "...Old things are passed away; behold, all things are become new" Now you are ready to tune your new Guitar.

I would like you to think of this book as a workbook or a lesson book. This book does not take the place of reading your Bible, attending a great church that preaches the word or fellowshipping with other believers. Also reading other materials, seeking wisdom from mature seasoned teachers and quiet time with God are essential aspects to our spiritual growth. What it will do if you practice the principles and wisdom presented, is it will amplify all of the above and help you play with your brothers and sisters more harmoniously. This in turn will multiply your impact on the world in which you live.

PARTS OF GUITAR AND YOU

Now let us imagine that you are the guitar made up of three basic parts. The body is made up of wood, plastic and other physical materials, much like or similar to your body. Terms such as the flesh, the outward man/woman, or some call it our earth suit, is the part that people see and you see when you look in the mirror. As a Christian, God refers to it as the Temple of the Holy Spirit. This part also includes our five senses; sight, touch, smell, hearing, and taste which we use to make contact with the physical world around us.

The second part is the tuning keys which you turn to make the strings looser or tighter to change the pitch of the strings. The part of you which these represent is your soul which includes your mind, will and emotions. These are part of what gives your flesh life and cause you to react or respond to what your senses pick up. There are a multitude of influences and experiences that affect your soul. Some of them are planned and we as individuals decide how and what we feed upon both intellectually and emotionally. Other influences are developed with no conscious effort of our own. Some of these are environment, family, friends and events. These we can also consciously make decisions about as Christians and it will determine how our strings are tuned.

The third part, and the part we will focus on the most are the strings. The strings represent the spirit or the inner man. This is where life and life more abundantly resides. This is the place that inside every person without Jesus, is empty. This is a void that can only be filled by the Holy Spirit, The spirit of God. It was designed by God for God. As children of God it is our responsibility to feed and fill this with His word, The Bible is the word which can only fill that hole. As we read and hear the word, the word goes down into our inner being and is digested and distributed as needed. It is similar to eating physical food. We don't know exactly how it works but it does. Some dietitians and doctors have a better understanding but still don't know exactly. The fact is that food gives us physical strength and power to operator more effectively in this world. Feeding on the word does the same thing for our spiritual man/woman. In the physical we take vitamins to ensure that we are getting all the minerals and vitamins that are needed. As we continue in the word (Bible) and use this workbook, it becomes a vitamin for the spirit.

The attributes of our Father can be found in the word. Therefore as we dig for the personality of our Father we will get a clearer picture and consciousness of who we are as sons and daughters of God. Also never forget what Jesus said "That if you've seen me you have seen the Father" and "The Father and I are one" These attributes are the strings which make up our inner man and personality. Jesus' behavior in situations will be used to show how the strings are to work when tuned properly.

Are we Ready to start tuning?

There is one more point and that is related to the amount of time in which each of you has been born again. That is, it doesn't really matter. You maybe a new born or you may have been born again for 30 years. The funny thing about guitars is that they can always be tuned better and clearer. The ones that have been left and not played for extended periods of time may need more work than the ones that are brand new.

Note: There will be notes throughout this book. They are tidbits of wisdom and knowledge that have been acquired over 27 years. They will help you tune your string and enhance your other Bible studies.

Now let us start tuning these strings. The strings which I chose were based on years of study, sitting under many teachers, teaching by the anointed word of God. There were many hours and days of prayer. Even then the choice of the final two strings was difficult. If we are to live by all the word of God and His attributes which are multidimensional and vast, then the task can be over whelming. To simplify we will be working on six strings in this work book. The method of grasping the concepts of each string can be duplicated. This will be explained in more detail as we begin tuning the six strings. Let's start with Love, Faith, Righteousness, Holiness, Authority and Anointing.

ATTRIBUTES OF GOD
Jesus is our example to follow!

The scripture (John 11:1 – 44) will be used to explain how the strings of our guitar sound when they are all operating in perfect tune: Jesus raising Lazarus from the dead, paraphrased.

Example: Jesus speaking with all six strings "Lazarus Come forth". Jesus loved Lazarus. Jesus is righteousness. Jesus thanked the Father before he spoke "Faith" He knew, without a doubt, that God would do what he said. Jesus is the word of truth and Life. He is holiness. "I am the resurrection & Life" He knows who He is and the authority that went with his person. Jesus had the fullness of the Holy Spirit "Anointing and Power".

In the final chapter when you understand that you are the guitar and your strings are in tune, then you will speak as Jesus spoke. The power of God will move and miracles will be. The world is the audience and the fields to be harvested. So flow in the spirit, make beautiful music in this world and you will be amazed. You may be thinking, what is this person writing about? After reading and doing what is presented in this workbook you will better understand.

God will play you with a multitude of other instruments to create an orchestra in the lives of many or just one.

Keep feeding on the word as you do this workbook. The revelation of who you are as a child of God will grow in maturity. You will begin to step out in Faith and do the works that Jesus did. Then God will take you to even greater works.

Note: There are many scriptures mentioned in each chapter and only a couple will be used. For your own benefit I strongly suggest that you read and meditate on all in relation to each Chapter.

STRING OF LOVE

We will start with the definition out of the Webster's Dictionary. This is the meaning of love which most people understand. Now when the word love is read in the bible; the word and the attributes described will enlighten our consciousness and expand the true meaning and depth of Love.

Webster's Definition of Love:

to regard with affection, to like, to delight in. To be in love; to be tenderly attached. Warm affection; fond attachment; the passion between the sexes, the object beloved a word of endearment. Cupid the God of Love; The score of nothing at tennis, etc.

The word love has been used in very diverse ways. From the intimate relationship between a man and woman to "I love ice cream" or "I love to go fishing". As a Christian the way in which the word is used in the Bible is vital to our understanding of God and His attributes [personality]. The world's definition and usage truly does not explain the attributes of my God. I believe Webster did not know love according to the Bible very well and his string was way out of tune. The sad part is most people think like the above definition. Now let us renew our minds and tune our string in line with God's word. The first step is to make a list of some of the scriptures on love.

Love As A Noun:

- Proverbs 10:12
- Proverbs 15:17
- Matthew 24:12
- 1 John 4:7-12
- John 13:35
- John 15:13
- Romans 13:10
- Ephesians 3:19
- 1 Timothy 6:10
- 1 John 4:18
- Revelation 2:4

Love As A Verb:

- Deuteronomy 6:5
- Ecclesiastes 3:8
- Matthews 5:44
- John 15:12
- 1 John 4:19

All of these scriptures use the word love in many different ways also. This may seem confusing but as we begin tuning the string of love,

the revelation of the word love will get clearer. Let us start with I Corinthians 13 which is described as the love chapter. The King James Version of the Bible uses the word charity.

Note: The word love and charity are inter-changeable in this case. In the King James Version charity is used and in the New King James, love is written rather than charity. This is just an example of why it is important to read different translations of the Bible to get a clearer understanding and tone.

Let's continue tuning the string of Love, which will take digging in the word. The first turn of the tuner is the importance of love. I Corinthian 13 1-3 states, *"I can have gifts of prophecy, tongues, faith and be a giver of all my things but don't have love. I have nothing."* Also in I John 3:14 it speaks, *"We know that we have passed from death onto life, because we love the brethren."* Galatians 5:14 says, *"for all the law is fulfilled in one word, even in this; thou shalt love thy neighbor as they self"* I John 3: 1,2 tells us, *"behold what manner of love the Father hath bestowed upon us, that we should be called the sons of God; therefore the world know us not, because it knew him not. Beloved, now are we the Sons of God."*

Note: God is spirit and the things of God are spiritually discerned.

God is Love. Turn until the string is sharp and clear; His attributes are expressed in the verse 1 Corinthian 13 4-8.

1 Corinthian 13 4-8:

"Love suffers long and is kind; love does not envy; Love does not parade itself; is not puffed up does not behave rudely, does not seek its own, is not provoked, thinks no evil; does not rejoice in iniquity, but rejoices in the truth, bears all things, believes all things, hopes all things, endures all things. Love never fails."

I Corinthian 13:13:
And now abide faith, hope, love, these three but the greatest of these is love.

Ephesians 4:32 & Ephesians 5: 1&2:
These scripture verses are to be looked up and read out loud which will also clear the tone of your string. Now, do the work and the rewards
are tremendous. Your string is almost in tune when you do some more digging and acting on the scriptures by confessing them. (This is saying them out loud to yourself over and over developing your inner faith.) Then search your heart to forgive any one that you may have ill feelings towards. Love one another with the God kind of love that dwells in you. Confess I am love.

Note: don't just rely on the index at the back of your Bible. It usually is incomplete and there are many more related scriptures then are listed. Do some research on your own and find a book written by an individual that has done a lot of digging.

Example: "Love the Way to Victory" by Kenneth E. Hagin

This is a book that touched my heart and catapulted my life to victory. You may list other books and materials that you use to help keep you in tune. Write them in this work book to keep a record for yourself. There will be a section at the end of each chapter for your convenience. Continue walking in Love on a daily basis, the word in you will grow.

Note: Ask the Holy Spirit to reveal the word before you even start to read the Bible. Let God know that you desire an intimate experience with Him. The Holy Spirit which lives within us is our main teacher.

Personal log

Dates Author / speaker # times read comment

7/1982-8/1982 Kenneth Hagin sr. 1985, 95,99,2000
'Love The Way to Victory' 3/2011
1982 attended a seminar speaker Hagin sr. Worcester auditorium opened spiritual eyes on love.

Add pages as needed

STRING OF FAITH

Faith (noun): Belief; trust, confidence, conviction in regard to religion; system of religious beliefs; strict adherence to duty and promises, word or honor pledged.

Scripture Verses:

- Matthew 9:22
- Mark 5:34, 10:52
- Luke 8:48, 17:19
- Matthew 17:20
- Luke 17:6
- Roman 1:17, 3:28, 5:1, 4:5
- Ephesians 2:8
- Hebrews 11:1
- James 2:20

Let us start with Hebrews 11:1 *now faith is the substance of things hoped for, the evidence of things not seen.* Let us think or meditate on that for a moment. Substance: That of which a thing consists; material; a body. Faith *"evidence of things not yet seen"* Hebrews 11:5

Example: *"By Faith Enoch was taken away... He pleased God... But without faith it is impossible to please Him, for he who comes to God must believe that He is, and that he is a rewarder of those who diligently seek Him."*

Hebrews 11:17:
By faith Abraham, when he was tested, offered up Isaac and he who had received the promise offered up his only begotten son

Hebrews 11:7:
By faith Noah, being divinely warned of things not yet seen, moved with Godly fear.

Note: Faith believes then acts and it is seen by God as Holiness, Righteousness and Obedience.

All of Hebrews is filled with examples of men believing God and acting on Faith. Hebrews 12:1&2; "Therefore we also, since we are surrounded by so great a cloud of witnesses, let us lay a side every weight, and the sin which so easily ensnares us and let us run with endurance the race that is set before us, looking unto Jesus, the author and finisher of our <u>faith,</u> who for the joy that was set before Him endured the cross, dispensing the shame and has sat down at the right hand of the throne of God".

This string is tuned by acting on the word. There are a multitude of good books, tapes and videos on faith. Have the faith of God or the God kind of Faith. Your local Christian book store will have many great materials on Faith and you may also find free materials from your local full gospel Churches or other churches that will help tune this string. If you are an older Christian like me, you have great reading materials on your book shelves which you have not looked at in years. Pull them off the shelves reread them when in the related chapter of this workbook. You will be amazed how the Spirit will enlighten you. WE ARE GETTING CLOSER TO JESUS'S RETURN. THE SPIRIT IS BEING STIRRED IN GOD'S CHILDREN!

Note: Read scriptures out loud over and over until they sink way down into your spirit. They will empower you to achieve greater success in every area of your life and reading out loud will help build your faith.

One of the processes or games that I like to play is finding and counting all the times that faith, or any other word I am studying, is in the Bible. Then I read a little before the word and a little after it. I do this quickly from verse to verse and the power of God's word begins to reveal God to me. You may have other processes or games that you use that help you get closer to your father. There are many ways to reach a maturity and relationship with our creator; this workbook is only one. You may disagree with points presented and that is okay.

Dates	author / speaker	# times	comments

This is your work book, be creative and personal!!!

THE STRING OF RIGHTEOUSNESS

Righteousness: Integrity; parity of heart and rectitude of life; justice; conformity to God's Will; Righteous; upright; pious just honest; virtuous; equitable.

Scripture Verses:

- Psalm 23:3
- Matthew 5:6
- Romans 5:17, 5:21, 6:13
- 2 Corinthians 5:20
- Romans 10:6-8, 12:10
- Philippians 3:8 & 9

Philippians 3:8-9:
yet indeed I also count all things loss for the excellence of the knowledge of Christ Jesus my Lord, for whom I have suffered the loss of all things, and count them as rubbish, that I may gain Christ and be found in Him not having my own righteousness, which is from the law, but that which is through faith in Christ, the righteousness which is from God by faith...

I used that scripture first to show that it is not our earned righteousness but is given to us by our loving Father [God]. He gives a gift, and we receive it when we receive Jesus as our Lord and savior.

Note: This is similar to being born into a natural family and automatically receiving rights, privileges and authority in that family.

2 Corinthians 5:20-21:
Now then, we are ambassadors for Christ and though God were pleading through us; we implore you on Christ's behalf, he reconciled to God. For He made Him who knew no sin to be sin for us, that we might (become) the righteousness of god in Him. (King James Version)

Suggested Reading: 2 Corinthians 5:16-21

Again he made a righteous Jesus to become sin so that we through Him may become the righteousness of God in Him. There are many ways in which this subject is covered in different denominations, churches and ethnic groups. The one that gives you clearer understanding to tune your string is correct. God does not honor any man or group over any other. His truth is truth! Many may be offended by the person or church that helps you, but the main issue is, that it is between you and God. My first experience with teachings on the subject was through the Catholic Church. Then in my later years I received great revelation of the gift of Righteousness through Kenneth Copeland's video called "Getting on the Right Road."

Note: Sometimes we need to cross denominational boundaries to fine tune our strings.

Now the string of righteousness is becoming clearer and in harmony with Love and Faith. These were present in both scriptures and reinforce that your strings are being tuned.

Note: You will find many of the strings in scriptures that you read. Again, I stress, when you read them out loud your Faith will grow stronger. Faith comes by hearing and by hearing the word of God (Bible).

At this point your consciousness of who you are in Christ Jesus is beginning to grow. The Holy Spirit inside of you is digesting the spiritual food as long as you take the time to dig, plant and feed. God's attributes are becoming your attributes as a son or daughter of God.

Dates	Author / event	# times experienced	comments
5/2011	video: Kenneth Copeland 'Getting on the Right Road'	8 excitement	watch again

Just like a guitar, you will pick this book up and tune yourself many times. Remember to place this workbook in a place, as you would a diary, which you will see and remember to pick it up. This may be the legacy that you leave to your children and theirs for many generations. Souls have been brought into the kingdom by such personal legacies.

Notes you want to remember (when I was watching the video my inside was excited)

STRING OF HOLINESS

The fourth string I planned was to be authority. Then I received a prompt by the Holy Spirit, 'change it to Holiness'. To better understand what is meant by a prompt: Bruce Wilkinson's book, **'You Were Born For This'** is a great tool and can be an inspiration to becoming a deliverer of God's miracles on a daily basis. He shares insight on the different ways God moves in our lives. God is moving every day to accomplish His purpose.

Holiness: State or quality of being Holy; moral goodness; sanctity. Holy; free from sin; immaculate consecrated, sacred.

Scripture Verses:

- 2 Corinthians 6:14-18, 7:1
- 1 Corinthians 3:17
- Romans 6:22
- Ephesians 4:24

I know this is an attribute of God because there are angels around the throne that sing 'Holy Holy Holy are you Lord', all the time. (Revelation 4:8)

Just listing the scriptures on Holy and Holiness your string will begin tuning.

- "Where on thou stand is Holy Ground." - Exodus 3:5
- "To keep it holy" - Exodus 20:8
- "be ye Holy" - Leviticus 20:7
- "not that which is Holy" - Matthew 7:6
- "against the Holy Ghost" - Matthew 12:13
- "The Holy Ghost descended" - Luke 3:22
- "Holy Ghost is come" - Acts 8:15
- "Comfort of the Holy Ghost" - Acts 9:31

- **Note** (‘Holy Ghost' and 'Holy Spirit' are synonymous.)
- “Holy Ghost teaches” - I Corinthians 2:13
- “temple of God is Holy” - I Corinthians 3:17
- “Temple is Holy Temple” “Holy and beloved” - I Thessalonians 5:27

Let us stop at this one for a moment: 1 Thessalonians 5:17-27.

Note: Sometimes you have to backup and read more than just that one scripture to fine tune your string, and also to see how it relates to your other strings. Throughout the rest of this workbook **Strum** will be used to help you understand how all the strings work together.

1 Thessalonians 5:17-28:
Pray without ceasing. In everything give thanks; for this is the will of God in Christ Jesus for you. Do not quench the Spirit. (This shows we have a part in our own Holiness). Do not despise prophecies. Test all things; hold fast what is good. Abstain from every form of evil. Now may the God of peace Himself sanctify you completely; and may your whole spirit, soul, and body be preserved blameless at the coming of our Lord Jesus Christ. He who calls you is faithful, who also will do it (faith). Brethren, pray for us. Greet all the brethren with a holy kiss. I charge you by the Lord that this epistle be read to all the holy brethren. The grace of our Lord Jesus Christ be with you. Amen.

Why did I write all this out? As an example, the more senses you use acquiring the word, the stronger your spirit writes with the Holy Spirit.

Note: Righteous is God's gift to us. Our Holiness is our gift to God. In the Old Testament and covenant, God was in the Holy of Hollies. The inner most room of the temple. In the new covenant, by the Blood of Jesus we are the temple of the Holy Spirit. We are to cleanse our temple (Body) so that God can live within us through the Holy Spirit (unhindered by sin). Therefore our communication and walk with God can be an intimate relationship and he can move with His power through us.

Strum: When holiness is combined with the strings of Love, Faith and Righteousness working harmoniously together, we really feel His presence. Our self-image is starting to take on the attributes of our Father. Our usefulness and effect in the world grows. Rivers of living water start to rise from our inner man.

Note: Never ever forget that we are all children of God and Jesus Christ is the Lord of our lives. We are not qualified to be Lord of our own lives. We are to fear (reverence) our Father which is the first step to wisdom. Be servants to one another and humbly respect the Holy Spirit that lives in each of us.

Dates	Author / event / relationship	location	comments

FIFTH STRING - AUTHORITY

Authority: Legal power or rights; influence conferred by character or station; person in power; testimony; credibility; precedent.

Scripture Verses:

- Mathew 7:29
- Mark 1:22
- 1 Timothy 2:2
- Thessalonians 2:15
- 1 Peter 3:22

Before we read Matthew 7:29 let us look at Matthew7: 21-28.

Mathew 7:21-29:
Not everyone who says to me "Lord, Lord" shall enter the kingdom of heaven, but he who does the will of my Father in heaven? Therefore whoever hears these sayings of mine and does them, I will liken him to a wise man who built his house on the rock: and the rain descended, the floods came, and the winds blew and beat on that house; and it did not fall, for it was founded on the rock. But everyone who hears these sayings of mine, and does not do them, will be like a foolish man who built his house on the sand: and The rain descended, the floods came, and the winds blew and beat on that house; and it fell, and great was its fall." And it came to pass, when Jesus had ended these sayings the people were astonished at his doctrine: ***For He taught them as one having authority, and not as the scribes.***

Note This is worth repeating: And so it was, when Jesus had ended these sayings, that the people were astonished at His teaching. For He taught them as one having authority, and not as the scribes.

Speaking with the authority which God had given Him, Jesus's words amazed the people! What Jesus spoke was and is the truth on which we can build our lives. That same power and authority is in us when we speak the word and will of God with the other four strings of our inner man.

A STRUM is when you PAUSE, MEDITATE and REREAD

1 Peter 3:22:
(Jesus) who has gone into heaven and is at the right hand of God, angels and authorities and powers having been made subject to Him.

Strum: Power and authority are linked together. To better understand authority let us take a detour and look into power.

Power: Ability to act or do; strength; influence, talent; command, authority; one who exercises authority; a state of government.

<u>Scripture Verses:</u>

- Proverbs 3:27, 3:18, 3:21
- Isaiah 40:29
- Zechariah 4:6
- Matthew 6:13, 28:18
- Luke 24:49
- John 1:12
- Acts 1:8
- Philippians 5:10
- 2 Timothy 1:7, 3:5

2 Timothy 1:7:
For God has not given us a spirit of fear, but of power and of love and of a sound mind.

Glory to God we have the spirit of power, His power, through the Holy Spirit which resides in us. Glory! This string is really getting tuned and sounds wonderful (Heavenly) with Love. God is love and God is Power and we are made in His image.

Strum: While looking up power in Philippians, my faith and righteous strings get tuned a little more (Phil 3:9). And be found in Him, not having mine own righteousness, which is of the law, but that which is through the Faith of Christ, the righteousness which is of God by Faith.

Note: This is how the words, which you are building within your spirit, just jump off the pages at you like metal to a magnet. That is the spirit within you feeding.

Luke 24:49:

And, Behold, I send the promise of my Father upon you; but tarry ye in the city of Jerusalem, until ye be endured with power from on high.

You may have already received your power by the laying on of hands at a special meeting or a church service or through a friend (in any place or at any time). If you have not just seek a place where there are believers and ask to have hands laid on you for the power. God is no respecter of persons and freely gives to those who truly ask from their hearts.

Matthew 28:18-20:

And Jesus came and spoke unto them, saying, *"All authority has been given to me in heaven and on earth. Go therefore and make disciples of all nations, baptizing them in the name of the Father and of the Son and of the Holy Spirit, teaching them to observe all things that I have commanded you; and, lo, I am with you always, even unto the end of the age." Amen.*

Note: Your world begins in your Neighborhood, Town or City, Work (do not witness while you are on employers time. You may be the witness through your being and actions), home, clubs, grocery store, etc.

2 Corinthians 5:17 and 5:21 gives us the right and authority to share with others.

2 Corinthians 5:17- 21:

Therefore if anyone is in Christ, he is a new creature; old things have passed away; behold, all things have become new. Now all things are of God, who has reconciled us to Himself through Jesus

Christ, and has given us the ministry of reconciliation, that is, that God was in Christ reconciling the world to Himself, not imputing their trespasses to them, and has committed to us the word of reconciliation. Now then, we are ambassadors for Christ, as though God were pleading through us: we implore you on Christ's behalf, be reconciled to God. For He made Him who knew no sin to be sin for us, that we might become the righteousness of God in Him.

Note: Foot notes of other scriptures are used to clarify the scripture with the use of two or more witnesses. (Rome. 5:10, Eph. 2:16, Col. 1:20)

Note: Have you noticed that there is less and less of me writing and more of God's word? This is because God's word has been planted in my heart for years on a daily bases. The Holy Spirit has a lot to work with in me. He gets all the praise for without the Holy Spirit we are just empty vessels. With the Holy Spirit we are powerful children of God.

The disciples received the baptism of the Holy Spirit on the day of Pentecost; they were in the upper room praying and in one accord. Spirit descended as tongues of fire, the whole place was shaken.

Now I will repeat what I stated just a page earlier, it is very important.

We receive when we ask! The Holy Spirit may enter us when hands of a believer are laid on us. We ask and receive by the grace of God through our relationship with Him. There is evidence that He has entered us by; the speaking in other tongues, revelation knowledge, healings and miracles in our lives. We get greater revelations when reading the Bible. The Holy Spirit is our main teacher. Now whatever is said in the word “The Bible” we can do by faith. God's word is the truth, only believe and obey.

Dates	Author / speaker / event	Comments

SIXTH STRING ANOINTING

Anointed: The Messiah
Anoint: to rub over with oil, to consecrate by unction

Scripture Verses:

- Isaiah 61:1
- Luke 4:18
- John 12:3
- 1 Samuel 26:9
- Psalm 105:15
- Isaiah 45:1

Jesus received the anointing after he was baptized by John and the spirit descended like a dove. Before that he walked and worked as a man for thirty years, a righteous man.

Luke 4:18:

The spirit of the Lord is upon me, because he hath anointed me to preach the gospel to the poor; he hath sent me to heel the brokenhearted, to preach deliverance to the captives, and recovering of sight to the blind, to set at liberty them that are bruised, to preach the acceptable year of the Lord.

Strum: Many revelations in our lives become part of our being when we least expect them. The above scripture became part of me while I was lying in bed and began pondering over it. Now you need to know that I did not bring this to mind, I was just lying in bed and allowed my thoughts to continue moving freely. Jesus was thirty years old when this took place. As a Jewish boy He must have been given a number of opportunities to read scriptures in public. What made this time any different than the others? The difference was that it was after He was baptized by John in the river Jordan. Then He spent forty days being tempted by the devil, He had become stronger spiritually. The Spirit was there but he only got stronger when his consciousness of it became evident through the temptations.

Acts 2:1-4:

And when the day of Pentecost was fully come, they were all with one accord in one place. And suddenly there came a sound from heaven as of a rushing mighty wind, and it filled the entire house where they were sitting. And there appeared unto them cloven tongues like as fire, and it sat upon each of them. And they were all filled with the Holy Ghost, and began to speak with other tongues, as the Spirit gave them utterance.

Strum: This was the first day that the Spirit of God entered men after Jesus rising. Man truly became the sons and daughters of God with the same Spirit that was upon Jesus now dwelling in them. Now you may better understand that God's attributes and character are ours. We are becoming more aware of this fact. You do not lose your individuality but rather you are enhanced with power and gifts.

The anointing is given to us so we, as Jesus, can be ambassadors from heaven to this earth, reconciling the world back to God. We are the healers of mankind. The out pour of power, the power of God is through anointed men and women, children of God. The flow of the Holy Spirit through us is directly related to all other five strings. They work and combine together to bring the power flow as we submit our will and desires to God's will and purpose. Our role is to be available and ask to be played to reach all those described in Luke 4:18. The times, places and miracles are all orchestrated by God.

Strum: Where ever we walk is holy ground because God is in us walking on this planet. Every encounter with another human being could be a divine appointment.

Dates	Author / relationships / events	Comments

ATTRIBUTES TO FOLLOW

Jesus is our example to follow!

Strum: Let us look at the same scripture now and see if you understand how it relates to the strings inside of you.

Example: Jesus speaking with all six strings "Lazarus Come forth". Jesus loved Lazarus. Jesus is righteousness. Jesus thanked the Father before he spoke "Faith" He knew, without a doubt, that God would do what he said. He was and is in constant contact with His father through the Holy Spirit and only did what the Father showed Him. Jesus is the word of truth and Life. He is holiness. "I am the resurrection & Life" He knew who He is and the authority that went with his person. Jesus had the fullness of the Holy Spirit "Anointing and Power".

When Jesus spoke, it was God speaking through Jesus as a man, God upon the Earth. We are by the gift of the Holy Spirit, God working on the earth. Now we are accomplishing His will as we walk in who we are in Jesus. We know His will, that all come to know Him and that His kids have a part in building the Kingdom of God, II Corinthians 5: 18 -20. Awesome! We get to take part in the process of reconciliation.

God will play you with a multitude of other instruments to create an orchestra in the lives of many or just one. All you have to do is to ask to be played. Then be obedient to move when he shows you what to say or do. Do not worry or get discouraged if and when you miss it. We have all missed it many times and will in the future. We in most cases do not even realize it until after God reveals it to us. God is big enough to correct our mess ups. I know from personal experience (over and over again). God gets excited when we as His children keep getting up, tuning ourselves more, become more sensitive to the leading of the Holy Spirit and get in a closer relationship with Him.

Now, are you ready for the piano? God is amazing and his personal attributes are diverse and beautiful. He also gives us many tools that we may use in our personal ministries. They all make up you. The more you are aware of them in depth, the more your character and personality expands. So let’s start with a few of my favorites Grace, Compassion, The Name of 'Jesus', Salt, Boldness, Humility, Covenant, Blessing and the list goes on. You choose the ones you want or need to work on, God will also help. He said that He would never leave us or forsake us. While we mature, we will by nature humble ourselves one to another and walk in Love, one to another. WE TRULY BECOME THE CHILDREN OF GOD!

Keep feeding on the word. The revelation of who you are as a child of God will grow to levels of maturity. You will do the works that Jesus did and even greater works.

Notes on times God touched you

This area is to record those times that God moved through you with a supernatural power for; Healings, words of knowledge, prophecy, Wisdom, discerning of spirits, revelation knowledge, Holy peace, Etc.

God's Touch

January 1, 2010, I had worked 11 PM to 7 AM on that New Year's Eve morning went to sleep at 7:45 AM.

Usually my wife woke me at 11 AM or near that time to have breakfast and get a few things done.

That morning was different, there was silent in the house, no voice calling to me and I was about to find out how different soon.

After rolling out of bed at 11:15 and not hearing anything I walked down stairs. I called my wife's name at the bottom, once then again. No answer! No coffee brewing and complete silence. Looking around down stairs my mind started to wonder and I quickly checked to see if the car was in the drive, it was. I continued the search, then! I saw her through the sliding glass patio doors lying on the deck. I Yelled NO!!! Through open the door. As soon as the door slide open I felt a bitter cold blast hit my face. I noticed a thin layer of snow that had melted around the motionless body. Quickly moving to check her for a breath and pulse, then lifting with my hands under her damp arm pits she slide out of my grasp. I caught her secured my grip and dragged her into the house.

At a frantic pace I checked he breathing, raspy but she was breathing. There was dried blood below her nose and I tried waking her. Shaking and yelling there was no response. Her cloths were dam and I was thinking warmth. After grabbing a blanket and wrapping it around her I ran for the phone. 911, what's your emergency? As I held the phone over my wife's cold pail body I told them. With-in minutes the EMT's and police were present. I remember sitting at the dining room table with the police asking me questions as the EMT's worked in the living room. Then the awful cold blue!, clear…clear…clear and then the frantic motion to get out of the house and into the Ambulance. Red lights, blue lights flashing everywhere and my brother running towards me. Questions then, do you want me to drive? I said yes. It seemed if I were in another world and this was just a dream. I don't remember much of the ride to the hospital.

As we arrived at the emergency entrance the red lights were off and the Ambulance was motionless. My brother and I were directed to a small room called the bereavement room where they put people when they did not expect the patient to make it. While sitting across from my brother I cried uncontrollable, and then I began to pray! The words of my pastor rang in my head about praying for the sick. Fervently and compassionately I prayed and prayed, mostly in tongues. Then I had a sudden peace enveloped me like a cocoon. It was wonderful! It is a total and complete peace where my mind could listen and my heart is at rest. There I had a vision of me walking into the emergency room where I saw my wife bundled up with tubes running out of her nose and mouth. There were people and equipment all about her. Slowly I walked towards her and a path opened up. Placing my hands on her cheers I spoke with all that was in me, "I Rebuke Death out of this body and speak life into it, In the Name of Jesus!" I knew at that moment that my wife would be alright. While basking in this peace I heard the doctor talking outside the half opened door. Getting up, my brother and I joined other family members in a circle around the doctor. He explained that her heart had stopped at least three times, her core temperature was 84 degrees and they had done everything that they could do. She still remained in a comma and suggested that she be moved to U-Mass medical in Worcester, which we agreed to.

When the doctor had finished I asked if I could see my wife. My mother-in-law asked at about the same time in this way, "Can I see my daughter one more time before she dies?" I could hear within myself 'she will live and not die' and found more comfort and peace. I was allowed into the Emergency room and it looked exactly as it had earlier in the vision. As I approached the staff and equipment were moved aside. I spoke with power and authority just as Jesus must have at Lazarus's grave. The Father had shown me what to do and I did it. I know who I am as a child of God and the authority flowed out of me. She did not die and is alive at the writing of this book. That peace remains in me and around me. The Love of God is powerful and can overcome anything that is thrown at us.

Nothing will separate us from the Love of God!

THE BEGINNING OF

An Instrument for God's Purpose

This book began with a bunch of ideas which I just jotted down on paper. The more I looked at the notes the clearer the direction and the outline of the book began to take form. This may not happen all the time but we are given tidbits of knowledge and ideas at a time. That is why the next note is important.

Note: When God gives an idea write it down at the times of inspirations. The following are some of the ones I wrote down before writing this work book. This is the way that this book got started. By listening to the still small voice that speaks to us from our inner being when we are quiet and listening.

Think in terms of a guitar (six strings) and you are the instrument
(Strings are attributes within you)

Love, Faith, Righteousness, Holiness, Authority, Anointing

Many of the questions and points made below will line up with your understanding. Also who we are in relation to our place and time on this earth becomes clearer.

Obedience to Holy Spirit "He says, I do"
Know His voice "God, Jesus, Holy Spirit" Inner witness,
Guidance, Word, Others
Love scriptures Preachers (Tapes & books),
Meditate, write down
Renewing Mind & Spirit Diligently

Les Paul Sunburst 1959 guitar 1,600 or 1,800 made 1,000 still NOT
accounted for worth $400,000 may reach $1 million
What is in a name reputation of beauty and sound quality?
Act: (respond) based on scriptures
Power Anointing
Holy Spirit working through us
God, Word, Holy Spirit Our Faith in Action

Is the action “spoken” based on the word?
YOU, Gods Word In Action

Another purpose of this book is to teach you how to dig for nuggets of truth. How do we develop a consciousness and revelation of who we are as children of God? To listen to the leading of the Holy Spirit within us, step out in Faith and enjoy the infilling power of God. To be a better instrument for God's will (purpose) to be accomplished and His enjoyment that His children (All His Children) are taking part in His Master Plan.

After you read this workbook, continue tuning your strings and reading the Bible. Also attending fellowship where the powerful word of God is preached will help your strings stay in tune. Also,very important are your one on one personal relationship with fellow Christians that have a desire to mature and do God's will. This will surely sharpen your sword. Every time you see or hear one of the words we used as strings they will jump out at you expanding your consciousness of who you are. Your faith, usefulness and all that you are, explodes as you continue maturing to the fullness of Jesus, the Anointed Son of God. You are that joy that was set before Him so He could endure the cross. Now you are an anointed child of God, along with many others, to continue the work that Jesus started.

CONCLUSION

God revealed that I was an ambassador for Him with the duty of reconciliation. I felt like Moses "who am I Lord: what do I say and what do I do. God pointed out that I only had to partner with Him and he would move through me. The anointed, that is you and I, we are like an electric guitar with the largest amplifiers you can imagine. When God touches those strings the power flows. Do not be concerned for what to say or do, just keep tuning your strings.

Is your guitar tuned? Let us play a little song together to check the tune of our strings and how they sound in a continual melody. The first stanza starts with you and your everyday being. The fact that the Holy Spirit lives in you (meditate on this fact, the part of God which went across the earth when God spoke, creating all the earth's beauty AND RAISED JESUS from the dead, also is the same Spirit that was working with Jesus as He walked the earth, is in YOU. Now is faith!! Holy Spirit is the master musician. With God as the conductor and Jesus as our advocate at His right side, we will perform with excellence, confidence and power.

Chorus: God loves me 3x

Now knowledge is power and you have started the process through your decisions to feed on healthy spiritual food. Now I hope you have gotten a good picture of the method of tuning your strings. This workbook was not to change you only to reveal that which you already are. It was only written to help you obtain the knowledge of the attributes of God that are already inside you. You already are the righteousness of God in Christ, a child in the family of God. The Movie "The Matrix" has a great scene when the star (Keana Reeve as Mr. Neal Anderson) goes to see the oracle to find out if he is the one to free the people of Zion. After a short conversation and a cookie, the oracle points to a saying written in Latin above the doorway. It said 'know thy self 'and with this knowledge his life begins to change. Now as you begin to know yourself as God's child, you become stronger. You become an Instrument for God's purpose. This does not happen instantly but as you walk, listen and are obedient you grow stronger.

Chorus: God loves me 3x

There is another revelation that hits as your consciousness grows of who you are as a son and/or daughter of God. That you are the epistle of Jesus Christ and that the story continues through you. That where ever you go and whatever you do with God is another chapter in the book of acts. Your place in the great story of creation is being written every moment of everyday and you are the star, as is every other individual in Gods Family. We together make up all the instruments in the process of bringing more and more into God's family. You are an ambassador for Jesus Christ to this world. Yes we are the ones to save the lost and continue the process which Jesus began.

Chorus: God loves me 3x

This book has inspired me to open other avenues to reach others. Also to give you an opportunity to share how God is using you as an instrument for his purpose. Our shared experiences will help others overcome and concur the forces of evil in this world. We will be the children of God which He desires. This will be done through a book "Instruments Being Played" and a website www.daviddesbois.com. Also, Now that we have the guitar tuned, how about the piano? The piano has 88 keys and multiple strings for each key. A few strings you may start with are: Grace, Peace, Hope, Covenant, Humility, Blessing and Abide. It is your instrument; you and God decide what strings need to be tuned. I will be working on some in my Blog, livinglovinglordsheart at Blogspot.com.

Walk with God and make wonderful music together with your other brothers and sisters. I know that the peace that surpasses understanding will be yours. God Bless and I hope that this book has touched your heart.

Chorus: We are alive! 3x

ABOUT THE AUTHOR

David J DesBois

Husband, father, grandfather, friend, brother and son

Resident of Baldwinville, Massachusetts

Humble servant in several churches for over twenty-seven years: usher, children s ministry, intercessory prayer, choir, Evangelist, and counselor

Helped start mission to Haiti, support missionaries and missions

Carpenter and builder, worked in social services with youth, adults, elderly, handicapped, and fellow Christians

Seed of Abraham, Isaac and Jacob   from the tribe of Judah lineage of David

Blood bought child of God through Jesus our Lord

An instrument for God's purpose

Just a regular guy

notes

www.ingramcontent.com/pod-product-compliance
Ingram Content Group UK Ltd.
Pitfield, Milton Keynes, MK11 3LW, UK
UKHW041837200726
13854UKWH00003BA/1189

9 781105 556371